Sleep Softly Now

Ian Assersohn

MUSIC DEPARTMENT

OXFORD
UNIVERSITY PRESS

Sleep Softly Now

Medieval English carol

IAN ASSERSOHN

* Gently re-emphasize the repeated notes without breaking up the line.

Duration: 3.5 mins

Printed in Great Britain

OXFORD UNIVERSITY PRESS, MUSIC DEPARTMENT, GREAT CLARENDON STREET, OXFORD OX2 6DP
The Moral Rights of the Composer have been asserted. Photocopying this copyright material is ILLEGAL.

X814 Sleep Softly Now ASSERSOHN

ISBN 978-0-19-355116-9

9 780193 551169

Printed in Great Britain by Caligraving Ltd, Thetford, Norfolk.